DIVISION STREET

# DIVISION STREET

Helen Mort

Chatto & Windus
LONDON

Published by Chatto & Windus 2013

6 8 10 9 7 5

First published in Great Britain in 2013 by
Chatto & Windus
Random House, 20 Vauxhall Bridge Road,
London SW1V 2SA
www.randomhouse.co.uk

Addresses for companies within The Random House Group Limited can be found at:
www.randomhouse.co.uk/offices.htm

The Random House Group Limited Reg. No. 954009

A CIP catalogue record for this book
is available from the British Library

ISBN 9780701186845

The Random House Group Limited supports The Forest Stewardship
Council® (FSC®), the leading international forest-certification organisation.
Our books carrying the FSC label are printed on FSC®-certified paper.
FSC is the only forest-certification scheme supported by the leading
environmental organisations, including Greenpeace. Our
paper procurement policy can be found at
www.randomhouse.co.uk/environment

Set in Minion 11/14 pt
Design by Ron Costley
Typeset by Palimpsest Book Production Limited, Falkirk, Stirlingshire

Printed and bound in Great Britain by Clays Ltd, St Ives plc

*For Les and Jan*

'I stood already committed to a profound duplicity of life . . . both sides of me were in dead earnest.'

ROBERT LOUIS STEVENSON, *The Strange Case of Dr Jekyll and Mr Hyde*

# Contents

# DIVISION STREET

# The French for Death

I trampled ants on the quay at Dieppe, dawdling
by the desk where they wouldn't take yes for an answer;
yes, it was our name and spelled just so –
Dad repeated it in Oldham's finest guttural,
we shook our heads at *Moor* and *Maud* and *Morden*.

Rope swung from the captain's fist
and lashed the water. I saw him shudder,
troubled by a vision of our crossing:
glower of thunder, the lurch and buckle
of the ferry. I looked him in the eye

and popped my bubblegum. Child
from the underworld in red sandals
and a Disney T-shirt, not yet ashamed
by that curt syllable, not yet the girl
who takes the worst route home, pauses

at the mouths of alleyways, or kisses
strangers on the nameless pier; eyes open,
staring out to sea, as if, in the distance
there's the spindle of a shipwreck,
prow angled to a far country.

# Twenty-Two Words for Snow

The lawn was freezing over
but the air stayed empty,
and I wondered how the Inuit
would name this waiting –
our radio playing to itself in the bathroom,
the sound from the street
of ice-cream vans out of season
in this town where we don't have

twenty-two words for anything,
where I learned the name
for artificial hills, the bridge
where a man was felled by bricks
in the strike. From the window,
I watch the sky as it starts to fill.
In the kitchen, dad sifts flour,
still panning for something.

# Deer

The deer my mother swears to God we never saw,
the ones that stepped between the trees
on pound-coin-coloured hooves,
I'd bring them up each teatime in the holidays

and they were brighter every time I did;
more supple than the otters we waited for
at Ullapool, more graceful than the kingfisher
that darned the river south of Rannoch Moor.

Five years on, in that same house, I rose
for water in the middle of the night and watched
my mother at the window, looking out
to where the forest lapped the garden's edge.

From where she stood, I saw them stealing
through the pines and they must have been closer
than before, because I had no memory
of those fish-bone ribs, that ragged fur,

their eyes, like hers, that flickered back
towards whatever followed them.

# The Judgement of Solomon

They pressed the knife
into my parting

and I cleaved
like orange-flesh.

My kind were never
whole:

one blue eye
for each lover

and a hand
for each to take,

my lips
twin promises,

and in its cage,
the heart,

a cloven hoof.

## Take Notes

You shut the door, drove me to the all-night shops.
I was three weeks late. The air was damp and hot.
Our pale reflections on the black windscreen,
the local radio DJ playing *Dancing Queen*
and the checkout girl in the superstore
who didn't look at me, just what I bought.
You pointed out each lit window in town.
*Take notes*, you said, *one day you'll write this down.*

It's true. Most days, I plunder what I see,
play deaf unless a poem answers me.
When I nod absently at what you've said,
I'm thinking of that night instead –
me in the bathroom, long before time,
already squinting for the telltale line.

# North of Everywhere

### 1 *Hermaness*

My body was a compass needle
guiding me past every place
I'd once called North: to Sheffield

and beyond, the sleeping giant
of Manchester,
then east to Aberdeen.

By night, I touched the edge of Unst,
the land bowing to meet the sea,
a lighthouse with no keeper but a gull,

the tide, dragged from a latitude
I couldn't even dream. I stopped
and let my heart go on ahead of me.

## II *Shetland*

Wind-whittled, turned on the sea's lathe too long,
built by a craftsman who can't leave it alone:
the trees scoured off, the houses pared down
to their stones, the animals less skin than bone.

We walk to Windhoose, find a barn even the ghosts
have left, a sheep's spine turning on a string,
a name reduced to nothing but its sound.
Our silences become the better part of us.

### III *Westing*

The coastline's fingers reaching for the sea
and mine for ledges in the sodden cliffs.

The dog finding the grey harp of a wing
or clenching a jawbone between her teeth
as if she's going to wring the history out.

The way those lovers on the clifftop path
must hug within an inch of life
until one of them confesses everything.

Below, an otter mines the water,
gets a single truth from it.

## IV *Aurora Borealis*

How typical of us: thinking that pale green corridor
cutting across the blacked-out Baliasta road
must be a searchlight, hunting us.

We clutched each other as we never would again
then skittered home, imagining
we were extras in a B movie:

the Shetland hills huge UFOs,
or the whole island a slumbering beast whose back
we clung to, this the beam of his mate's eye.

We looked down at our steps along the track
and missed the sky's brief fire, the North
lighting its own touchpaper and standing back.

# Fur

Snow wants my childhood for itself.
It wants to claim The Blacksmith's Arms,
digest the Calow Fish Bar whole. Snow's tongue
has found the crevices of Eastwood Park.
It licks the war memorial, weighs down the trees

and everyone I knew is sinking past their knees.
On Allpits Road, the family dog is swallowed neat.
Snow gets beneath my schoolfriends' clothes
and touches them until they freeze, and still
it wants the long-abandoned Working Men's Club,

hollows where bar stools scuffed the floor.
It moves to fill each empty glass behind the bar.
On Orchid Close, I stand to watch it fur the driveway
of a man who's lived in the same bungalow for thirty years
and dreams of digging his way out.

# Stainless Stephen

He haunts the chippies mostly,
nodding his approval
at the puns: *A Salt & Battery,*
*In Cod We Trust.*

He's dressed up to the nines
in stainless shoes, a plated vest,
two spoons for a bow tie. A fork
to comb his sleek, black hair.

He says: *I'm aimless comma*
*brainless comma Stainless Stephen*
*semi-colon semi-conscious*
*ordering my chips full stop*

And when the shop lads
shove him out into the cold,
he knows a pub across the river
where the doors will never shut,

a shell between the empty works,
where brambles twine around the pumps
and every glass is draped
with webs. Where men stride in

still sweating from the braziers
that vanished thirty years ago
and tug their collars,
loosening the noose of heat.

The jukebox hasn't changed its tune
since '71. The landlord stands,
a statue at the bar, as Stainless
saunters in and tips his silver hat,

surveys his audience –
the roughed-up chairs, the yawning
window panes, the shabby walls
that echo back each joke

as if they know them off by heart.
Semi-quaver, semi-frantic,
Stainless croons the golden oldies,
sing-alongs to sway to,

here in Sheffield
where they drink till dawn
and beg for encores, know
there's no such thing as *Time*.

# Fagan's

Themed quiz, the host part-drunkard, part-Messiah,
his long hair lapping at his mustard tie.
I'm trying to connect everything with fire:
the page reads *starter, cracker, fighter, fly.*

My pints of Moonshine and my team of one.
The strip lights catch the table like a spark.
I turned to ask you something and you'd gone.
The windows frame their version of the dark.

Halfway down West Street, you'll be lighting up.
*What links the fire of London and the colour blue?*
I'm wondering if a match would be enough
or if there's really no smoke without you.

# Rag & Bone

Seeing the cart and quartz-white mare
from your window, open to the street,
I want the things that other people don't:

tortoiseshell glasses someone must have
died in, a boa's glossy soddenness,
the china mug, cracked with a final argument.

I want to climb inside the knackered stronghold
of a fridge – no longer cool – or lie beside you
on a mattress moulded by another's bones,

drift down the City road, lay claim
to every disused shop, the winter trees
still reaching out for all the leaves they lost.

Come back: we'll take the slim, once-wanted moon,
unfashionable blackboard sky. No-one will miss
the world tonight. Let's have the lot.

# Oldham's Burning Sands

Sundays were *Last Train to Dobcross*,
*Sit Thee Down*, the blunt crescendo
of *On Oldham's Burning Sands* . . . That dead
half hour between The White Hart kicking out
and tea left cooling on the kitchen tabletop,
our front room brimming with *the orange groves
of Werneth*, long guitar solos that sounded
like a cardigan unravelling in Saddleworth.

My dad conducted from the floor. And mum,
you should have told me grandad's street in Oldham
smelled of Sarson's Vinegar, not coconut,
that people sing the sweetest when they're drunk.
But thank you for my ignorance, those nights
I'd mouth approximations of the words,
lie down beside the palm-leaf-coloured couch,
the small sun of the hanging lamp
and burn.

# Scab

A stone is lobbed in '84,
hangs like a star over Orgreave.
*Welcome to Sheffield.* Border-land,
our town of miracles – the wine
turning to water in the pubs,
the tax man ransacking the Church,
plenty of room at every inn.
And watch: a car flares
into a burning bush.

\*

A stone like a star over Orgreave,
a spat-out word that can't be taken back.
They follow it: the bobbies from ten counties,
pickets up from Markham,
down from Cortonwood,
the cavalry, the fifty-eight Alsatian dogs.
They find the houses cold as barns,
the whole town gathered in the street.
The wise men. Shepherds. Beasts.

\*

*Star of Orgreave, star of light, star
of fucking royal shite. Westward leading,
kids want feeding, guide us to your
perfect light.* One brings a half-brick,

one brings a shield, one brings
a truncheon, one a chain. *Bearing gifts*
*we've travelled so far. God*
*or fuck knows who we are.* A man foetal
beside the railway tracks.
Anointment of blood.

II

On New Year's Eve, the dead end of 2003,
my Cambridge offer sits untouched
for hours amongst the bills.
I drink the old year out in Calow WMC,
my breath sickly with Malibu and coke.
Someone is falling from a stool or kissing
her way round the Miners' Welfare football team.
At midnight, I join a conga line that ends
where it began. At 2am, I walk back
past the landfill site, my steps
ruining the snow's unopened envelope.

\*


My college room is opposite
a gown-hire shop. Next door, a girl
sings opera all afternoon, stops once
to ask me where I got my accent from.
A Chinese woman enters carefully,
empties the bins without a word.
I sit behind my polished desk
and watch the dusk disguise each shop,
the corridor in silence till my neighbour
trills back into life again. Day
after day, I cannot learn the tune.

III

This is a reconstruction. Nobody
will get hurt. There are miners playing
coppers, ex-coppers shouting
*Maggie, Out.* There are battle specialists,
The Vikings and The Sealed Knot.
There will be opportunities to leave,
a handshake at the end. Please note
the language used for authenticity:
example – scab, example – cunt.

*

This is a re-enactment.
When I blow the whistle, charge
but not before. On my instruction,
throw your missiles in the air.
On my instruction, tackle him,
then kick him when he's down,
kick him in the bollocks, boot him
like a man in flames. Now harder,
kick him till he doesn't know his name.

*

This is a reconstruction.
It is important to film everything.
Pickets chased on horseback into Asda,
running shirtless through the aisles of tins.

A lad who sprints through ginnels,
gardens, up somebody's stairs,
into a room where two more miners
hide beneath the bed, or else
are lost – or left for dead.

IV

After the challenge of the cutlery,
a vial of prime-cut-coloured port.
Stand up. Then nod from left to right,
mutter the Latin underneath your breath
not knowing if it's thanks or blasphemy
and pass it anti-clockwise with a final nod.
The trick's in moving artlessly,
not faltering as if it burns
your hands. Now sit down.
Keep your silence.
Don't spill a drop.

\*


Summer is fish-tail ballgowns,
free champagne, a wine
everyone else is able to pronounce,
a man who steers me to a table
lined with oysters, marble-blue.
I taste metal first, then brine. And soon,
I'll slip beneath the surface of the night,
hold my breath, count the underwater lights
until my boyfriend hauls me up again,
pulling at my hand and smiling,
telling me how far I've come.

## V

Years on, we'll make a blockbuster
from this: a film that gives the town
its own brass band, cuts out
the knuckles fringed with blood,
grafts in a panorama of the Moors.
This is our heritage: an actor
artfully roughed up, thirty years
of editing to keep the landfills
out of shot.

*

*They scabbed in 1926. They scabbed
in 1974. They'd scab tomorrow
if they had the chance . . .*
A loaded silence in the corner shop.
The painted fence, the shit
pushed through your letterbox,
your head-down hurried walk,
a backward glance that meets
a dead man's stare, unbroken
from three decades before.

*

One day, it crashes through
your windowpane; the stone,
the word, the fallen star. You're left

to guess which picket line
you crossed – a gilded College gate,
a better supermarket, the entrance
to your flat where, even now, someone
has scrawled the worst insult they can –
a name. Look close. It's yours.

# Carnation

They've built a Body Shop
in the old butchers' district –
caul and pig skin giving way
to coconut oil, jojoba,
as if the cloying air
should remind us
there's no such thing
as a simple kindness –
like the spring carnations
fetched from earth to market stall
and, while you wait, beheaded
for your buttonhole.

# Pit Closure as a Tarantino Short

*after Ian McMillan*

The Suit who pulled the trigger left
a card between the victim's fingers,
printed white on red.
*Business Closed* was all it said.

He wiped his bloodless hands
down his shirt for show,
as if someone still watched him
as he turned to go. And as he did,

he met the dead man's stare
and noticed how the bullet hole
between those two dark eyes
made a black ellipsis; then he swore

he heard the dead man's voice
above the heartbeat of the clock:
*Nothing's finished, only given up.*
Before he left, he checked the lock.

# Carceri d'Invenzione

*after Giovanni Battista Piranesi*

At the height of illness, Piranesi sketched imaginary
prison cells. *The Sawinghorse. The Pier with Chains.*
His hands moved with a fury so exact

it seemed his fever was condensing on the page.
*The Man on the Rack*, his one wild eye;
*The Giant Wheel*, a ferris turning on an absent hinge

and others, more innocuous; *Staircase with Trophies,
Rounded Tower*, inviting us to peer in close
and note the claustrophobic lines,

each walkway leading back towards
a darker focal point where we might watch
our own unlikely dungeons form:

I looked in, found *The Maze of Ponds, The Room
of Infinite White Tabletops, The Prison of a Thousand
Coathangers* where all thoughts are triangular,

until a small brick house appeared
and I squinted through its windows, saw
a room rinsed in sunlight where a man

much like my father sat transfixed by
the spin and judder of the washing machine:
chainless, free, unable to get up.

# George, Afraid of Fingerprints

Their gauze
was on his bookshelves, from the heartwood
to the spine of Henry James. They trailed him
as he clutched the banister at night.

At length
he thought of how they'd linger in the auburn
of his first wife's hair, their savour
on her temples, or her own quick fingertips,

imagined
them on patted dogs, the purple leaves
of late geraniums, or gathering ancient
in the pockets of his winter coat

then saw
them spread through every hand he'd shook
and every shoe he'd forced, still laced
onto his foot, and every door handle

he'd tried,
found locked. The shape of them
when he closed his eyes was like something
jammed at the dresser back,

a vision
of his childhood street, the varnish tin
in the corner shop, its silver lid,
the weight he pocketed.

His mother's voice.
The careful turning out and owning up.
Even now, his prints there in the centre,
brilliant spirals, burning.

# The Girl Next Door

First, she came to borrow sugar. Sunday afternoons
she'd cadge a pint of milk, sometimes a cigarette,
then greet the sunset in her overgrown back garden,
blowing smoke rings into mine. Soon she took

the unripe apples from my tree or asked for books
with tattered spines that caught her eye. I'd smile and nod.
She'd ring the doorbell late at night. I kept my curtains
    drawn,
the bathroom window lidded with a blind,

and taking out the bins I'd see her silhouette
in her kitchen, head tipped back, the way I stand.
Once, she turned to look me in the eye. These days
she wears her blonde hair short. I find excuses

not to leave the house; the evening rain,
the biting wind. Last night she said my name.
It suited her.

# Night

A karner butterfly,
climbing the stairwell
of late evening,

through the shadows
cast by larches, up
into the last colour

this sun can give;
how it holds
its black-edged wings,

unreadable. At night,
I take a leather book,
switch off the lamp

and open it. So dark,
I barely even see
the white. It's then

I settle on the bed.
It's then I read
just what I like.

# The Complete Works of Anonymous

I'd like to find it: leather-bound, unlikely
in the small-town library, somewhere
between Abbs and Ashbery, pages curling
like a song: *On Glasgow Rain, A Kiss for Marilyn,*
*The Hidden Life of Honey Bees,* a hundred titles
that I'd seen in old anthologies, wondered
at the hand behind them, said that word aloud –
*Anon. Anon,* a kind of lullaby.

I'll raise a glass to dear *Anonymous*: the old
familiar anti-signature, the simple courage
of that mark. I wish that each of us
could put such trust in words we'd spend a lifetime
on the vessel of a single verse, proofing our lines,
only to unmoor them from our names.

# White River Junction

In the museum-without-proprietor,
we found fourteen dead cockroaches,
a knife blood-coloured with old jam,
a jar of silt kept from the flood of 1926.

Beneath the fox's head that leered
down from one wall, there was a letter
covered by a wig, a leather dog collar
and a photograph of us, aged ten.

We didn't recognise the house –
its slant roof almost Scandinavian,
a bone-white Daimler on the drive –
but that was your face, that was mine:

we wore blue dungarees, our eyes
narrowed against the sun. The trees
looked like the trees that lined the roadside
here, in this forgotten corner of Vermont.

You grabbed my arm. An engine broke
the silence of the afternoon. If I could,
I'd remember your breathing. The crickets
whispering. The white car pulling up outside.

# The Year of the Ostrich

'A crane standing amidst a flock of chickens'
— CHINESE PROVERB


We've lost the zodiacs that show it,
perched between the rooster and the dog,
a slender neck craned to the east,
dark plumage snug above its legs;

or else it never made the chart
although it raced across
that mythic river, just behind the pig
or in the slipstream of the horse;

or waited on the bank
and, fearing water, gazed over
to where the other creatures stood
in line before the Emperor;

for surely there must be a sign
for those of us with such unlikely grace,
who hide our heads, or bear the weight
of wings that will not lift us.

# Thinspiration Shots

### I

Beneath the website's banner – *if you eat*
*you'll never dance again* – a close up
of a ballerina, veins like wires,
balancing on a single satin shoe.

Once, you dreamt of being small enough
to fit inside your grandma's jewellery box:
the dancer spinning on her gold left leg,
a mirror doubling her, the tinny music playing

on and on until the lid was shut at last,
and you were locked in with the dark.

### II

One model has a waist just like a snake.
The other is all whippet ribs,
her legs a deer's. The way she
rests one hand against the fence

hummingbird-light, as if she's never still,
reminds you of those hours of press ups
when the lights were out,
the dizzy sit-ups before dawn,

the miles you ran from home, near fainting,
trying to give yourself the slip.

III

Scroll down. A brunette in a mermaid pose,
too slight to break the surface of the lake.
You would have drunk a lake-full if you could,
those days they put you on the scales,

your bladder swollen, taut.
When they were sure there was
enough of you, you'd go upstairs,
lock the bathroom door,

crouch above the cool
white bowl and piss it all away.

IV

The shape of her is surely made for air,
the blonde who stands on the hillside,
back bared to the camera.

You take her in, those shoulder blades
sharpened to wings. You wanted to be light like her.
But now, your mirror's not a magnifying glass.

She teeters on the edge of flight. Tonight,
you look away. You close the page.

# Miss Heath

At seventy, our dance mistress
could still perform
a perfect *pas de chat.*

Her French was wasted
in the north. We stood in line
repeating *parr-durr-shat*

or sniggered
as she waited in the wings,
her right hand beating time

against her hip, her eyes
avoiding ours. She never
made the stage.

It took me twenty years
to understand. Alone tonight
and far from home

in shoes that pinch my toes
until they bleed, my back
held ballerina straight,

I wait as she did, too afraid
to walk into a bar
where everyone's a stranger,

see her glide
across the city night
to meet me, tall and white

and slim. A step behind,
she clicks her fingers. Elegant,
she counts me in.

# Beauty

'. . . is nothing but the beginning of terror' – RILKE

When Beauty stumbled down my road, tapped at my door
I saw her from the lounge and hid – her eyes were raw
from smoke, her cheeks like dough from where she'd wept
and worse, I didn't like the company she kept:
a red-faced drunk who towed a dachshund on a string.
Her mouth was slack. She never said a thing,
just stood and waited, dropped ash in my rose bed,
though as they walked away, she slowly turned her head.
For all she had a face made delicate by rain,
I told myself I'd never think of her again.

Besides, I spent the next year drinking in The Crown.
One Saturday, I rose to leave as they sat down.
She wore a hat. Her eyes were brighter than before
(although I didn't doubt that it was her I saw,
the stale light slung across her shoulders like a shawl,
her silhouette drawn sharp against the wall),
and though I grabbed my coat, I stood and stalled.
I knew I had to ask what she was called.
At last she spoke. I felt my hair rise all the same:
it's not the face we shrink from but the name.

## Other People's Dreams

The lives you have in other people's dreams
are lives no less. Tonight, for instance,
you are kissing the proprietor of SPAR

in a store room full of oranges. A school friend
has you kneeling in a layby of a mountain pass,
grappling with the front tyre of a truck,

and though your hair is jet black for disguise,
you are the photographer in your mother's
nightmare, angling the camera at her door.

Each morning, you must gather up these lives
and hold them tight, walk carefully downstairs,
slow as the girl in your own brief dream

who clutched a dozen long-stemmed roses
to her dress, until they merged
into a bloodstain on her ruined breast.

# Sleep

An auditorium
where nobody is clapping.

You enter naked, breasts
like two grey stones. You have
to leave your things outside.

They will be counted, weighed,
put back exactly as they weren't.

# Grasmere Oak

Last night, its shadow was the only thing
between you and the leaking dark,

the rain set loose and needling the bark.
Close up, its leaves direct the wind.

This is the landscape's hidden hinge
where all things start and peter out:

summers you were blind to, winters when
the tree gave back the tin-roof-coloured sky,

the small white knuckle of a distant farm.
These branches force the valley's arm,

pin down the light, headlock the air
until there's nothing left of it at all.

Watch how the leaves balance the sky,
then let it fall.

## Division Street

You brought me here to break it off
one muggy Tuesday. A brewing storm,
the pigeons sleek with rain.
My black umbrella flexed its wings.
Damp-skinned, I made for the crush
of bars, where couples slip white pills
from tongue to tongue, light as drizzle,
your fingers through my hair,
the way you nearly sneaked
a little something in my blood.

At the clinic, they asked if I'd tattoos.
I thought about the parlour
with its jaundiced walls, the knit-knit whine
of needle dotting bone, and, for a moment,
almost wished you'd left your mark;
subtle as the star I cover with T-shirts,
the memory of rain, or your head-down walk
along Division Street, slower each week, pausing
by the pubs, their windows so dim you see
nothing but your own reflection.

## Litton Mill

Hold me, you said,
the way a glove is held by water.
Black, fingerless, we'd watched it
clutch a path across the pond,
never sure if it was water or wool that clung fast.
The mills are plush apartments now,
flanked by stiff-backed chimneys
and you ache for living voices,
the clank and jostle of machinery,
for something to move in this glassy pool
where once, you were the waterwheel,
I, the dull silver it must
catch and release
and cannot hold.

# Outtakes

## I

You taught me longing is a matter
of suggestion: how the best directors
keep the climax of the heroine
off-screen and train the lens instead
on something like her black stilettos
standing empty by a doorway,
or the far side of her bed. How,
in *Fitzcarraldo*, Herzog lingers
on a close-up of a leopard cub
who scrupulously licks each paw
while, out of shot, a couple
tangle on a hammock bed,
laughter falling quiet.

## II

By now, I understand the concept
of the close-up perfectly; its use
in film noir, the camera
panning slow across a tidy desk
until it settles on some ordinary prop –
a letter-opener, a length of garden twine –
and draws so near we see each possibility,
the sharpened blade, the tightening cord.
It's all a matter of perspective.
*Look close enough*, you told me once,
*and anything's significant.* This morning,
when you showed me to the door,
your fingers touched my elbow for a second.

III

My favourite kind of shot?
A view of other people's windows,
glowing on a terraced street at night.
I pass their sickly yellow light
those evenings I walk home alone
and can't help glancing in to note
the invitation of a chair pulled out, the neck
of an anglepoise, the fresh cut daffodils
that finish off each perfect set, where, any second
you might saunter in to take your place
and turn your head, but not to look at me.
Perhaps you're startled by a cat outside;
your wife calling from another room.

# End

At night,
our shadows tangle

in their fatal dance.
Death is

the shape
beneath romance

and coming
is *le petit mort.*

I understand.
I've died already

by your hand.

# Seven Decapitations

### I

I creep up behind you
as you kneel at prayer.
You never see the knife. My hand
clutches your hair.

### II

We're lit by candles
from above.
A halo round your weeping neck.
A single dove.

### III·

Our image captured
in a prince's picture book.
I turn the page. I'll touch,
but I can't bear to look.

### IV

I'm a hitman and you
owe my boss a grand.
Before I leave, I change
my shirt and wash my hands.

V

I've put your head
back on again. It doesn't fall.
I'm a flower-arranger
in a dark church hall.

VI

Shakespearean: I give a speech
before the deed is wrought.
*Ah, what's a head*
*except a purse for thought?*

VII

This is the last time,
and the first time you shout.
I wish I'd done it quickly
while the lights were out.

# The Rorschach Tests

### I

In the unstoked embers of an open fire,
you see livid redcoats, bloodhounds

primed for quarry,
the fierce, mute breath of horses.

All I see is the cindered shape
of a hare, streaking through flames

to imagined safety. We can't tell
who is gaining ground.

### II

There is an artist who draws
patent leather shoes as mussel shells.

If a shoe can be a mussel shell,
how am I to know my face

from its own reflected alabaster?
Some nights I glance behind me,

back into the old French doors
and can't be sure which way

I'm turning; into the room,
or out into the glass.

## III

I can't pass a child in the street
without feeling ancient.

I can't overhear a song
without being silenced.

I stand at the junction,
watch the traffic lights

change amber to red.
Think of them,

there at midnight,
changing for nobody.

# Thread

From now, your movement
is a kite's: you have the sky
and yet you're tethered
to a man below, an ancestor

who looks on silently
from an old print: your face
in his and his in yours.
Even when he yields the string,

he's set your course. The breeze
may intervene, but you are lifted
by a finer thread, like all the living,
anchored by the dead.

# Fox Miles

Supple as a dream I can't call back,
a vixen, in the hedgerow's
matted black, is startled out
to skirt the dawn, and vanish with the dark –
her flame-bright tail extinguished
by the railings of the park. But first,
she bolts across an empty road
and keeps her pace with mine. I slow
to look at her across the gap. We run in time.

She turns her face. Her eyes flare
in the artificial light, and then
she finds a trapdoor in the night;
a corridor towards the sun that she
slinks down alone, and covers miles
she might mistake for home.
And what she sees she cannot tell,
but what she knows of distances,
and doesn't say, I know as well.

# The Dogs

Some mornings, waking up between the sandy whippet
and the black – their breathing slow as mine,
their eyes more sorrowful – I remind myself I'm not a dog.

It's not acceptable to taste the grass or roll in moss until
I'm musked with it. There are deer in the woods I'll never see.
My thirst discriminates. It does not have me bend

my grateful head to puddles, gutters, hollows
in the rock. I don't track rabbits in my sleep.
I'll not know love like theirs, observed in mute proximity

and if I sometimes sit bolt upright after dark, sensing
a movement in the yard, it's only that I've learned
a little of their vigilance. I'm not like them:

one night I'll set off past the meadow, down
behind the beck, beyond the blunt profile of Silver Howe
and nobody will call me back.

# Coffin Path

Who'd jog along the Coffin Path?
Most evenings only me,
hurrying between

the huddled trees,
boulders streaked with rain,
the bowed heads of the ferns,

on stones worn treacherous
by centuries – men shouldering
the dead from Ambleside.

Today, the dark's grown courteous:
shadows seem to step aside
to let me pass,

just like that summer afternoon
in Cambridge, when a hearse
gave way to me near Jesus Lane

and I sprinted on, noting the driver,
black-capped, glancing at his watch,
certain he'd overtake before too long.

# Items Carried Up Ben Nevis

The piano, that was easiest, despite the keys
rattling like dice beneath the lid, so next
I strapped a toffee-coloured horse across my back,
ferried a coffin with the body still inside
pitching from left to right with every move.

I took a statue of Napoleon and set it
on the pony track – a kind of shrine –
and goaded later in the pub, I dragged
the whole place up with me, stopped
to pull a pint beneath the summit cairn.

By then, the town was a skeleton,
the mountain curtseying with weight,
which just left you: I draped your arms
around my neck. Light as you are,
I couldn't take you with me. Not a step.

## Brocken Spectre

You say you've never seen a Brocken Spectre
haunt the ragged Scottish hills behind you,
never turned your head as you climbed alone

and seen your silent likeness in the mist,
drawing close. No double, tracking you up Blaven
and Sgurr Alasdair, those lonely peaks you loved.

But now the doctors talk of murmurs
in your heartbeat; irregularity, an echo
like a second pulse, hammering in your veins.

Dad, if you can't run beside me anymore,
keep pace with me up Kinder Scout, Win Hill,
Black Rocks; if you can't climb the pockmarked face

of grey Mam Tor, think of me as your Brocken Spectre.
Know that as the blizzards lash the tops,
I'll still be out there: gaining height,

I'm running up the frown-lines of the hill,
I'm keeping to a track
you pointed out to me ten years ago.

# Common Names

Somewhere, there is a spider called *Harrison Ford*,
another genus known as *Orson Welles*. The ocean's full
of seahorses who take their names from racing champs.
Above our heads, a solitary *Greta Garbo* wasp takes flight.

Each day, someone adopts a killer whale or buys
a patch of moon only to call it *Bob*, and last night,
watching meteors sail drunk across the Grasmere sky,
you told me there are minor planets christened

*Elvis, Nietzsche, Mr Spock*. Forgive me if I looked up
past your face, to see those nearly silver drops
make rivers in the dark, and, for a moment,
thought there might be stars named after us.

# Lowedges

And if those doors to other worlds exist

you'll find them here: Lowedges, where the city
smooths its skirt down in the name of modesty,

picks up its jacket, calls it a night. Here, bichon frises
chase their tails all morning on the astroturf,

a biker lets go of his handlebars and doesn't fall,
a woman rolls the afternoon into a cigarette

and smokes it silently. Forget the Cornish sea,
the top of Nevis with its trapdoor light . . .

If you're to leave this world, you'll leave it here:
this salvaged Friday, shop lights dimmed. Look up –

how easily the rain bisects the sky.

# Notes

'Scab' – The clash between police and picketing miners at Orgreave in 1984 remains one of the most iconic and controversial battles of the Miners' Strike. In 2001, conceptual artist Jeremy Deller staged a re-enactment of the events of June 1984 on location in Orgreave, featuring eight hundred people, many of whom were ex-miners or police involved in the original encounter.

'Stainless Stephen' – Arthur Clifford Baynes (1892–1971) was a comedian from Sheffield who performed under the stage name Stainless Stephen. He would appear dressed in a tuxedo, a rotating bow tie and a stainless steel vest. His trademark was his peculiar intoned monologues.

'Pit Closure as a Tarantino Short' was inspired by Ian McMillan's poem 'Pit Closure as Art'.

'Night' and 'Thread' were initially inspired by reading translations of the Russian poet Arseny Tarkovsky (father of the filmmaker Andrei Tarkovsky).

'Thinspiration Shots' – In 2010, twenty-eight-year-old Isobelle Caro died from respiratory problems associated with anorexia nervosa, having fought tirelessly to highlight the disease's dangers. Within hours of her death, her image had appeared on 'pro-ana' websites – sites which promote anorexia as a lifestyle choice and often feature 'thinspiration' images of emaciated women.

'Seven Decapitations' was written in response to a piece of artwork by Tom de Freston and first appeared in *Ekphrasis* (Freewood Publications, 2010).

'Common Names' – *Calponia harrisonfordi* is a species of spider discovered in 1993 and named after the actor Harrison Ford to thank him for narrating a documentary for the Natural History Museum. There are a number of other animal species with similar nomenclature, including a variety of slime mould beetle, *Agathidium bushi,* named after George W. Bush.

# Acknowledgements

Acknowledgements are due to the following publications, in which some of these poems first appeared: *Poetry Review, The North, The Rialto, The Morning Star, The Echo Room, Acumen, Spectator, Poetry Wales, Magma, Poetry International, Blackbox Manifold* and *Agenda*. Some poems are taken from my tall-lighthouse pamphlets 'the shape of every box' and 'a pint for the ghost', and also from 'Lie of the Land' (written during my tenure as Poet in Residence at The Wordsworth Trust).

As well as thanks to Parisa Ebrahimi at Chatto & Windus, I owe a debt of gratitude to Jacob Polley, Alan Buckley and Andrew Forster for their extensive editorial work, wisdom and patience.

Thanks also to Ian Cartland, Kathryn Daszkiewicz, Andrew McMillan, Graham Mort, Benjamin Morris, John McCullough and Ben Wilkinson for their editorial input on some of these poems or early manuscript drafts, and a huge thank you to Les Robinson at tall-lighthouse and Michael Bayley in Cambridge. Thanks to Tim Wells for advice on the ghost poems. Thanks also to my friends, particularly Jess and John, Grace and Iain, Ed, Dacia, Jamie, Bill and Rich, and my family: Janet, Andy, Clare and Beryl.

A further thank you to The Wordsworth Trust and to all at Christ's College, Cambridge for their encouragement over many years.